AMAZING OCEAN LIFE

# Seahorses

by Colleen Sexton

Kaleidoscope
Minneapolis, MN

**Where the Quest for Discovery Begins**



*Kaleidoscope Publishing, Inc.
6012 Blue Circle Drive
Minnetonka, MN 55343*

*Library of Congress Control Number
2022937341*

*ISBN
978-1-64519-563-4 (library bound)
978-1-64519-633-4 (ebook)*

**Bigfoot Jr. lurks within one of the images in this book. It's up to you to find him!**

# Table of Contents

# Under the Sea

Seahorses curl their tails around plants. They hold on in the flow of the ocean.

Seahorses are small fish. They can be green, blue, yellow, and other colors.

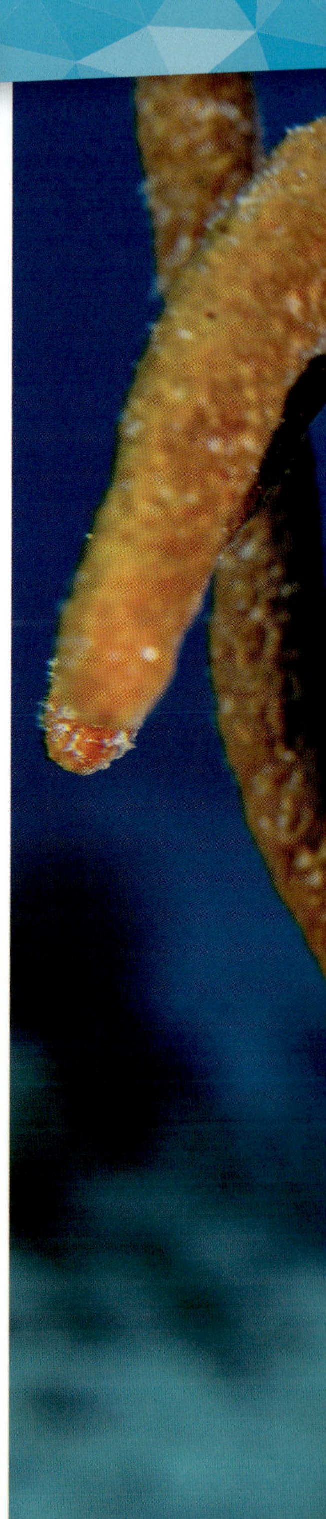

# Where Do Seahorses Live?

Seahorses are found in oceans around the world. Most live in warm waters near shore.

**Many seahorses live where rivers and oceans meet.**

Seahorses swim in **coral reefs**. They hide in seagrass and between rocks.

# From Head to Tail

A seahorse's head is shaped like a horse's head. That's how it got its name!

A seahorse's eyes can look in two different directions.

The seahorse has a small mouth. It is at the end of a long, narrow **snout**.

A seahorse breathes through **gills** near the back of its head.

Skin covers the hard **plates** that are all over a seahorses body.

The small **fins** on a seahorse's back help it swim.

A seahorse wraps its long tail around a plant to stay in one place.

**Seahorses swim slower than any other fish.**

# Parts of a Seahorse

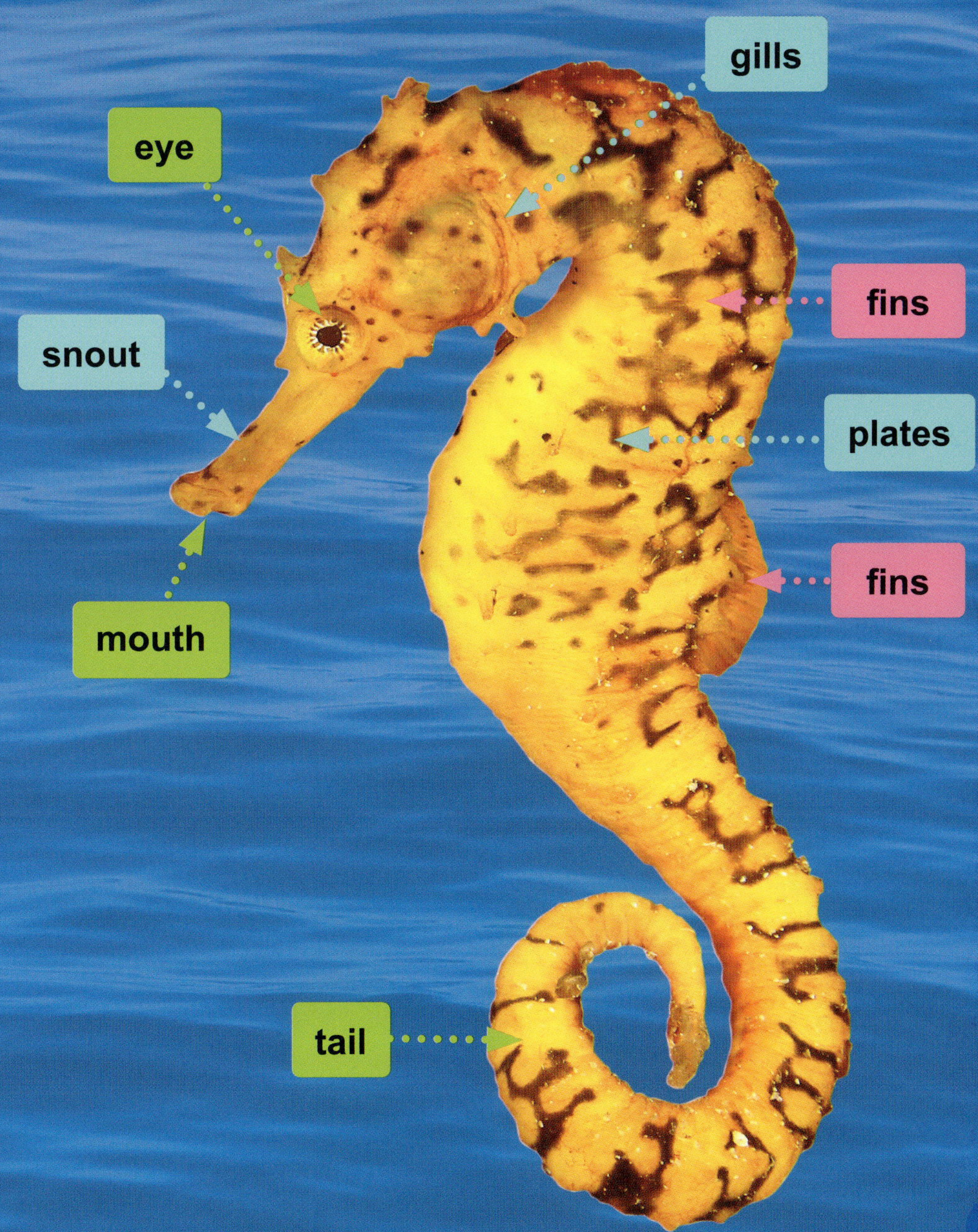

# Predator and Prey

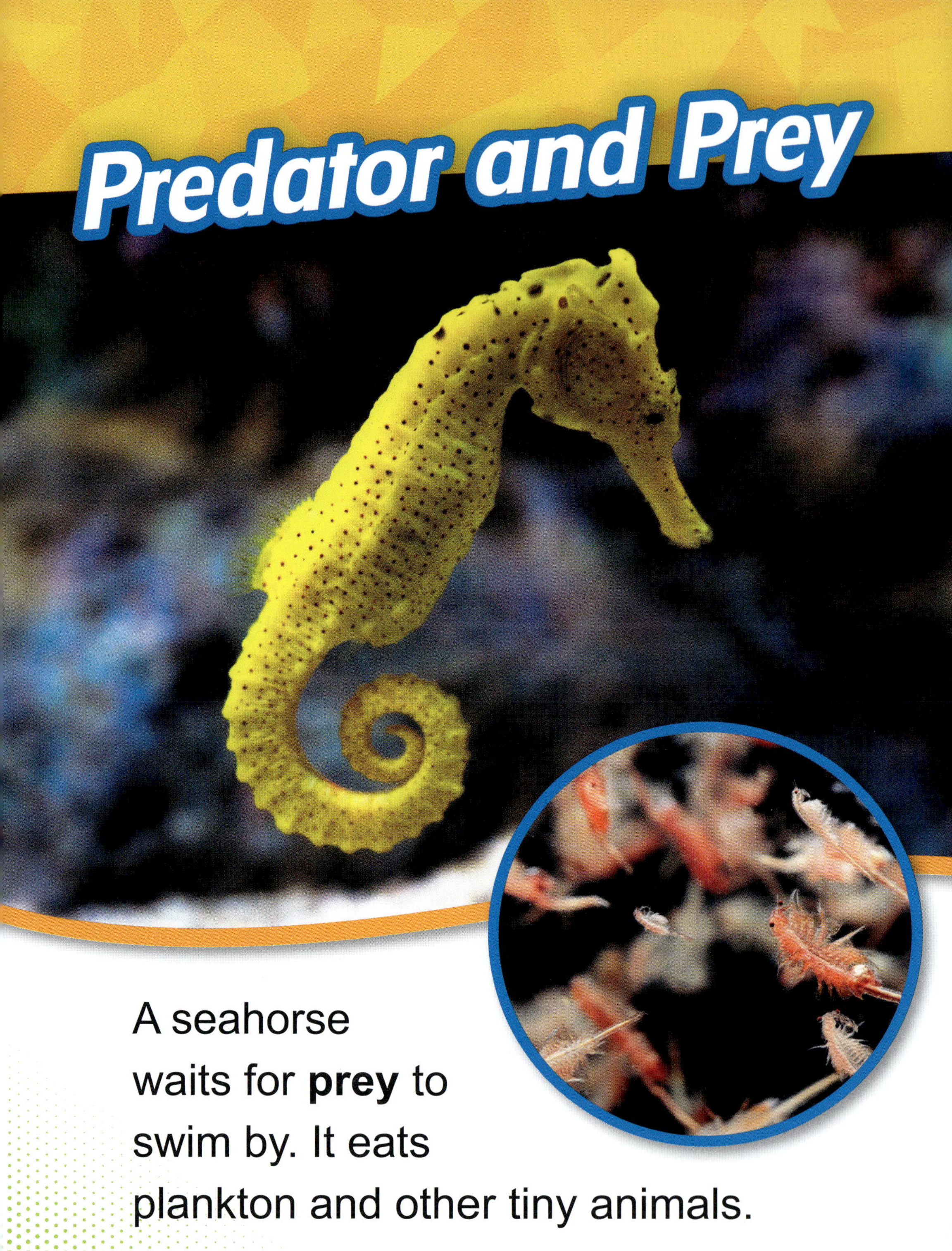

A seahorse waits for **prey** to swim by. It eats plankton and other tiny animals.

*Slurp!* The seahorse sucks the prey into its mouth and swallows it whole.

**Seahorses are always eating. They do not have stomachs to store food.**

Other animals hunt seahorses. A seahorse hides from **predators** to stay safe.

**FUN FACT**
**A seahorse isn't a favorite food of most of its predators. It has too many bones and not enough meat!**

A seahorse changes its color to match its **surroundings**. It fools the predator!

## What Eats Seahorses?

**skates**

**penguins**

**rays**

**sea turtles**

**tuna**

# Baby Seahorses

A female seahorse lays eggs. She puts them in a **pouch** on a male seahorse's belly. The male seahorse watches over the eggs.

The eggs hatch and the pouch opens. Hundreds of baby seahorses pop out of the pouch!

The babies float in the ocean for a while. Then they find their own place to live on the ocean floor.

# Photo Glossary

**coral reef:** A form of rock made of old and new corals. Seahorses swim in coral reefs.

**fins:** Flaps on a fish's body used for moving and steering through the water. A seahorse uses small fins on its back to swim.

**gills:** Slits near the mouth that a fish uses to breathe. A seahorse breathes through gills near the back of its head.

**plates:** Flat pieces of a bony skeleton on the outside of the body. The seahorse's plates are rings that go around the body.

**pouch:** A flap of skin in which animals carry their young. A male seahorse carries the eggs in a pouch on his belly.

**predator:** An animal that hunts other animals for food. A seahorse changes colors to hide from predators.

**prey:** An animal that is hunted by another animal for food. The seahorse swallows its prey whole.

**snout:** The long front part of an animal's head that makes up the nose and mouth. The A seahorse's snout is a long tube.

**surroundings:** The area around something. The seahorse can change color to match the plants, rocks, and coral around it.

# Read More


Bodden, Valerie. *Seahorses.* Amazing Animals. Mankato, MN: Creative Education, 2019.

Moening, Kate. *Sea Horses.* Animals of the Coral Reef. Minneapolis, MN: Bellwether Media, 2022.

Zommer, Yuval. *The Big Book of the Blue*. New York, NY: Thames & Hudson, 2018.

Factsurfer.com gives you a safe, fun way to find more information.

1. Go to www.factsurfer.com.
2. Enter "Seahorses" into the search box and click 🔍
3. Select your book cover to see a list of related websites.

# About the Author

Colleen Sexton is a writer and editor. She is the author of more than one hundred nonfiction books for kids on topics ranging from astronauts to glaciers to elephants. She lives in Minnesota.

## INDEX



## PHOTO CREDITS

The images in this book are reproduced through Shutterstock: Guy Shapira 3, 22; Nantawat Chotsuwan 4; Drew McArthur 5; Rattiya Thongdumhyu 6; katherineobrien 7; Makarova Viktoria 8; Vojce 8; Sahara Frost 9; Big 5 Studio 9; Robert Buchel 10, 22; Elena_sg80 11; GOLFX 12; Rich Carey 13, 23; Napat 14; Basicdog 14; Mike Workman 15; Laura Dts 15; tank200bar 16; Medvedeva Oxana 17; vladsilver 17; Nataliya Taratunina 17; maya_parf 17; lunamarina 17, 22; Arunee Rodloy 17, 22; Sahara Frost 18; Nicolas Primola 20; Nicole Griffin Ward 21; Carolina Marcias 21; Irina Markova 22; lanaid12 22; Kristina Vackova 22; Charlotte Bleijenberg 22; Songquan Deng 22. Cover: Rich Carey, Willyam Bradberry, Solarisys.